DREAM'S HOLD

poems by

Emily Saunders Nguyen

Finishing Line Press
Georgetown, Kentucky

DREAM'S HOLD

To Narrative,
for its varied attempts
to embrace Lyric

ACKNOWLEDGMENTS

Publisher: Leah Maines

Editor: Christen Kincaid

Cover Art and Design: Nam Nguyen

Author Photo: Nam Nguyen

Printed in the USA on acid-free paper.
Order online: www.finishinglinepress.com
also available on amazon.com

Author inquiries and mail orders:
Finishing Line Press
P. O. Box 1626
Georgetown, Kentucky 40324
U. S. A.

Table of Contents

PART I / Dream's Hold

PART II / Checking on Dream's Hold

PART III / A Rough Draft

PART IV / What Lies in Store

Comment on the title, DREAM'S HOLD.

A ship's hold. The tenacity of dream. The tenacity of the dream-like discontinuity of our lives...

As I reach near 70, this is my attempt to let the old Buddhist ideas seep in—every moment is a death. Every moment, a celebration. I try not to lose hold of the concepts of ephemerality and interdependence, but if I fall back, it just goes to prove the point; nothing lasts. They say that what is on the minds of the dying is love. I'm precocious in that way and love is always on my mind. But all this is just another instance of dream's hold.

I am a hybrid. Half Buddhist, half Christian, half a devotee of Bhakti, half a devotee of Chance—I don't even add up to myself. I'm 51 percent Jewish, 51 percent Moslem. I side with every side of myself. I wanted to wrap this up in Buddhist teachings. But it's just too neat. You'll see me siddle over into Western notions of love. You'll see me toe the line of basic Buddhist truths, like ephemerality and interdependence.

I have not grown in my understanding so much as gone out and come back to the starting point again. Deepening grooves along the way. It's an old song. What is life about? Love and receptivity, no doubt. No doubt, but what is love? Our lives are its proof.

I grasp after East. I grasp after West. Every moment is a death, every moment is a celebration.

In a sense, I'm trying to transpose a medieval Japanese set of ideas into a modern and western context. I think of the psychological worlds created in the Shinkokinshu, Hyakunin Isshu, but also in the Kokinshu, 300 years earlier, and wonder what Teika and Tsurayuki would say in the world of the 21st century. Their truths (ephemerality, emptiness) paradoxically are eternal. So perhaps they would proceed without blinking an eye, straight into our context.

I think of poetic series as a sort of conversation between the poems. One topic for awhile, a long time even; then reflections on it, changes in it, changes of topic, which can come so fast they are summed up by 'an avalanche of dreams.'

In the Seasonal poems of the Kokinshu (Heian Period Japan, c.905) you have, say, 8 poems about plum blossoms. One has come across a whole grove of them and notices them so deeply that later, 'one here, one there' becomes a significant recurrence of plum. I hope reading my poems in a series is like walking through a landscape.

Emily Saunders Nguyen

PART I

Dream's Hold

THE FATE OF THE HOURS

Twelve in the daylight,
Twelve at night.
The hours are your disciples.
You give them wine.
They offer you their tabula rasa—

You are lord of what you were
born into, lord of the senses.

Even the sense we call 'sense'—
You are lord of all that,
and our master, say the hours
though it was time itself
that you had mastered

and your very body that teaches
the hours their passage...

Each day I am sacrificed again
and the wine is tossed out,
says each hour in turn.

The hours miss the hours spent,
—spent at your beck and call.

The world's ambiguous.
Like the beauty of ivy
wrapping around a tree.

You opened up
a world in which
they flourished,
but to which
they can never return

—that is what they took away;
that is what they learned.

THE NOTE

Ivy chases
its lichen image
up the trunk
of the holly tree.

Only its thorns
persist
in their native brown,
where white ovals

gentle on the leaf
overlay
the green
of the holly.

Ages pass.
Meanwhile, snow...
A Paradise Lost
in Conversation.

Where have you buried
your thoughts of me?
Under what tumulus?
In what land?

THE RIPPLES AND THE WIND

The rabbit of a wind
lifts up leaves here,
slightly lowers
a small branch there

It nibbles holes
for itself
to go through.

Out on the lake—
How the little things
resolve themselves—
by growing larger,
by traveling far—

till at last
through the faultline
of touch, or proximity

through momentum
or what momentum forgot,
they clash
into some other design.

THE EARTH WE WALK ON

The earth we walk on
can be furled, unfurled—
a butterfly's wing
that carries light and shadow.

wings open each time a universe begins
—when they close, it is only as brief as a dream—

As for mind—Backpacker,
he's at home wherever he alights
among the myriad shapes of this shifter.

Sweet origamic, lover of mine,
stopping only for a moment in this world
or the next—moving on is your constant,
what figures come out of you!

SHADOWED

In your silence,
I am shadow.
All grows dark.
I loom larger and larger,
My bounds break.

Then, I see the world—
free in the light of itself.

Why am I standing
in these ruins?

THE PEACE OF THE PUZZLE RE-SOLVED

You are the irritant
in my mollusk shell—
guarding your distance,
while time polishes away...

Let's divest ourselves
of all this and begin again, you said.
(I mistook you)

I mistook you, and now
you are mine.

THE ATLANTIC

There is no door to the ocean.
A craze of ocean against the shore.

When he embraces you,
Ocean also embraces

far anemones,
stony coasts, starfish draped in kelp

seven miles leeward, rocky inlets,
a scalloped scarf—

For healing, the ocean's own saline solution.
The lifting up, the transposition...

Enter where you will,
you are completely engulfed

in the shape shift of the waves,
salt, its assault and savory.

HALF IN DREAM

In this woodcut,
this tapestry,
the naive truth
sets out.

Later
other truths
step out.
—They use
each other
as shields.

In Jacob Landau's
woodcut,
the truth steps over
various
pastel-colored
body parts.

In her fiber art
Hanneke de Neve
has the truth
step back.

The truth surveys
 with his feet,
with his eyes.

TWILIGHT

I took my place
between night and day
not knowing they were
incompatible worlds.

Day and night
seated at the table.

The clink of glasses,
an intimate gravity.
Colors spilling
And then, disjuncture.

You were a current

in a darkness
that leads to
a greater darkness.

I was dusk on the river.

You were the current
and I was dusk
and I was thinking
"...bear with me."

SUNRISE

Shading, more shading,
a type of bas relief.
Let light speak

its easy piece.
I crave
the way it carves a view.

Meaning steals out
of our words and hangs,
a jacket on barbed wire.

The moment, brittle,
shiny, magnetizes.
We live its force.

Life
in the open
clash of time.

Meanwhile light has
carried along with it
its underbelly.

It diverts
the world
into being.

SNOW HAS EMBELLISHED THE PLOT OF EARTH

Left and Right,
Spring justifies itself

March, with its limited
vocabulary of leaf

An occasional swallow that dips
through the indented air

Wrap around
and you are back

I want to follow you into the spiral binding

IRREGULARITIES

The day is a soufflé.
Without your even heat, I could
not prevent its falling.

*

In April, in my yard
the land moth emerges from
a chrysalis of snow.

*

Spring's
rave review of
the earth.

*

The sky is shifting
and mixing, preparing
its rain.

WHERE FIRE LIES

Spring sleeps
in the colors of dawn.
—She awakens into blossom.

Her landscapes speak Hiroshige:
brown, green, a touch of blue.

They also speak
the other end
of the spectrum,

but haltingly,
or half in dream.

Summer sleeps
in the curl of certain
winter branches.

In the crackle
of the fiery autumn leaf.

Fire lies in both
Summer
and in Autumn.

Summer says 'I will embed it'.
Autumn says 'I will embody it,

show its mirror
to all, and take
its essence away.'

Then Autumn piles up
its insomniac dreams

while Winter sinks
beneath the earth,

awakens,

then falls asleep
in the breezes.

ON DREAM

All night
we bail out
from the flood
of the day's
imaginings.

You are right
to sleep through
until afternoon.
Though I love
 the morning,

it is my coldness.
Marie-Eve stands
at the ironing board,
pressing
the coral colored

band, evening out
the wrinkles
of the day before.
Her sole
desire:

to escape
the parenthesis
into which
she had
been put.

Rain chases
the wind,
pelts down,
but its prey
is gone.

SUBJECT MATTERS

The others are chipping away at the ice
that holds us together
that slows down the distance between us.

Outside, light slips over icy branches
and skids into the square of light.

All the evidence of the world at large
is laid at my door:
the wind, the integrals of wind.

Asleep, I feel myself being moved over
one decimal place.

THE MODERN WORLD

Oh goddess of the night
why this slice of life?

render me rare, tender.

    *

I am tone deaf
to emotion.

    *

Let me run down
your schedule
like an eye
on the train,
its departure.

    *

I am tired
under the weight
of two images.

Pressed like the foot
of Buddha
into the open air.

MOODS AND CONFRONTATIONS

What do I want of you? I speak
like a water table rising. Where Flotsam
meets Jetsam and makes some notes.

*

Today is a shirt that's too big
for me. I squirm around within it.
There is always a sleeve over my face,
an armpit governing the motions of my hand.

*

I walk the shape of your
morning memes, hedges cut
to topiary, their odd organic
moves towards the sun
curbed into your space.

*

What lies between
my sand
and your waters
defines a line
that is not us,
but of our making.

*

Dreams escort me.
You are not pleased with my retinue.
You command a change of clothes.
Dreams turn inside out.
Loose ends hold them in place.
You are satisfied:
The Emperor of the Insides of Embroidery.

THE OPEN SLEEVE OF LOVE

I swirled out of you like snow:

light's crawling out of itself,
light tumbling into its own garden.

Your letter is on my desk.
Day's in its running stance, breaking through
the broken chord of night.

Rain clouds
once again tear open the mask
of Heaven.
The light moves its blossom
from tree to tree.

Love,
and the
open
sleeve
of love.

FALCON HEART

Not a shadow,
but a shadow's dream.

Why this impression
of an impression?
...no fine filigree...

Hawks fly through
the blue rooms,
the white rooms. They
thread through the green.

The underbelly
of a hawk
is its everyday
face.

Greyed, with
such a beauty...

The rhododendron
throws its color out
to the tips of its petals.

The falcon heart
is divided among the leaves.

Fret.

Fret, like
the wind
among the
roses.

IN BUNRAKU BLACK

I love reflections, their blatant stealth
of other vistas, other rooms…

And where mad truth can be addressed.

A line may be a harbor.
The old questions, oars.

I want to gather my asides

and see where they have taken me.
(some dark corner of false alarm?)

Then shadows will move
like puppeteers in Bunraku black.

They'll move along an avalanche of dreams.

PART II

Checking on Dream's Hold

THE ORIGIN OF DREAMS

In the early evening
the day calls out
"I am being left behind."

Night is buried deep
in his own thoughts.

Soon Day's
second thoughts
begin:

"I don't know what halls
my words echo down

—what I invade
in the heart
of the invader..."

As the sun
goes down

on every syllable
consonant
with desire

the cold grows
more penetrating still.

Day breaks down,
and says more
than she should:

"I will speak
through you

as fire
speaks
through wood."

CHECKING ON DREAM'S HOLD

Ironing out the seam
between awareness and dream

I ran to mother

a night sky that sits on
its prickly eggs

'Celestial Darkness', 'Mother Hen'

now hatching the light
by which I navigate

she had a well proportioned hand

continual lists; blueprints—
she always started out

what others could then finish

she could detect in a person's voice
the least resistance to task

set things soaking—

as a bird picks at the ice of the air
with its quibbling note.

Her Persian tablecloth

with its yellows and blacks—
why is what is embedded there
so embedded in me?

 the way an arrow strains through the air—

the sideways motion of
a yellow jacket alighting.

WORLDS APART

The prism is a box. We all lie in it sometimes.
It contains the catalog of all possibilities.
Yet it is itself emblematic of choice.
Context rules. Context is the Ruler.

You and I are the country's scribes.
We deal as well in lesser infinities.
With what's in play.
And interplay. Flexibility is the Ruler.

But: I know this. You know that.
It's all in the interstices.
There is often a trompe l'oeil
between perception and reality.

> Yes! Cambium
> is where the life
> of the tree is,
> not in memory storage.
>
> The life of truth
> is like the bark of a tree,
> between outer and inner worlds.
> ...I notice you doing a lot of waving.
>
> The wave is the art of balancing depth
> and surface. You want to communicate,
> but not too much. Mind can pick
> its way through chaos.
>
> But mind must also act as a shield.
> A human shield against sorrow.
> Between our minds and this matter,
> god speed the negotiations.

Perhaps you'll draw me out again.
Out of the box. The prism I keep myself in.

All that is past tense, past tortured, past the tremble.
But I lean on what I like.

And what I like is trust.
I'm in the prism as I speak.
Not sure I'll have access, though.
Trust is one of the larger infinities.

       We meet only in the Kaleidoscope.
       Interference patterns can be complex
       and beautiful. My district, my precinct,
       I'm paying you heed. Love is the tithe.

Mozart's Adagio from KV488
is a splendid world, a fine
world to explore and inhabit.
But we must add to it Mozart's K526

and 'How fragile we are',
(Stevie Wonder's rendition)
Cultivate your native madness.
But also aerate your thought—

for each of us is
compounded, co-founded, each
with their own compartments
and confinements.

       All is fine when we stand startled,
       having dropped our shield of scorn.
       But when we stand on the battlefield,
       we all stand on the battlefield blinded

       by our own standards. My standards
       are high here, low there,
       can even keep me from seeing
       whose feet are on what ground.

My dear, my one-deaf-ear,
ideal standards would be lowered
or raised at will—What tack to take
with you?   Consciousness is like a coordinate

or consciousness in its many forms
is like a set of coordinates.
The universe is messy
and has to be divided up somehow.

>*Charity:*
>*The ability to step into*
>*the fire of someone else's words*
>*and come out properly glazed.*

But it's a china that breaks.
There is yet a future to come. But if we
are still alive and yet not actively
headed back deep into the past...

>*Our god has abandoned us.*

>*We wander now*
>*In the wilderness alone.*

>*It was supposed*
>*to be a garden.*

>*A gift to the*
>*Homeless?*

>*No, a garden. Something*
>*To be kicked out of,*
>*Into something*
>*Else.*

The Sun is gorgeous, no doubt,
because it is bidding us goodbye.

THE NEW WORLD MEETS THE OLD

Here at the dock,
Do we harbor each other?

Or do we row into
the riff between us?

Do we alight on the moment:
a butterfly drunk with propulsion?

Why do I always
find myself in your boat?

The spectrum of me—
the coat of my many colors?

Or I find you distraught.
And myself distraught, I lose you.

Still, the image engages,
oil spill as proof.

How many dreams
are in my hold?

Is your boat a ship?
What will pass for navigation?

My darkest dreams
are punched through by light.

Awake in the darkest
part of night.

OCTOBER

Spring and Summer fall
all over themselves
to reach you, frail October.
In the light of your leaves,
the sun retreats,
and the moon takes on
too many shapes,
more than its thin crescent
can hold
without waxing bold all over.

In the ink winding through the inner chapters
there's an occasional flamboyant spill—

Remember when you walked into me?
I stare at my umbrella
as if your sense were rain
actually touching the body
of where I am.

THE CULT OF AUTUMN

The whole world is a-tilt
with expectation.

The gods have arrived
and are leaving their trace elements.

We have waited
like the vapor

—at this point never sure
we would condense once more

into what we were—
Soon, like the water

that courses
through autumn field and hollow,

we will find ourselves
brimming with color...

THE TURNING OVER OF THE EARTH

1. God said there was a Tree of Knowledge..
   "So Knowledge is an apple" said Eve.
   God prohibited eating from that tree.

   What if each thought
   were to ripen
   apart from the others
   and fall
   and spoil on the ground?

   He had his reasons.

2. Day is a specific green.
   Night draws an analogy.
   Day navigates by.
   Night draws another analogy.

3. There are closed words
   and open words.
   When you fill in the blanks,
   you must leave them open.

4. The hand we have been dealt
   is a royal flush.
   Our hand is full of spades.
   All is rank in the garden.

5. Within the X is the Y.
   We are nearing the end
   of the alphabet.
   The letters grow heavy
   and lie in each other's arms.

THE AYE AND WE-WAY OF THE COMPUTER AGE

We are engaged, when we are engaged,
in the (problematically engaging)
practice of EN.

1) To en-gage someone or something
is to en-site them, that is

a) to place them
at the center
of your attentive stare.

b) to locate them
in castles in the air
(this takes an all inclusive narrative stance
and is rather allusive).

c) in a flurry of wiki type action
to bring them together
with their of-the-moment confreres.

2. Here you will find the place
of the flutter of each and every leaf.
    The butterfly names for things.

    Here, I am speaking in the voice
of my dear dear dear. That is, I am speaking
from inside the voice of an old profess-or,
very much alive within and without me.

The butterfly searches for its comrade leaf.

COMPOSITION BY THE WINDOW

1. Of course it's unfair.
Brother image
waiting in the wings...

My psycho-somatic wanderings...
Broken sky!
You open

Yet where is my heart
in all this?
I cast the question.

It acts its part.
It lives the theater
of its own being.

As you do too, my love
—an intrusion, if you will,
on reality here.

2. The Truth
may be yours,
not mine.

But still, you hover,
you, the place of incipiencies—
you, the post-incipient.

Potentials fight like greenery
to come forth into the light.

a puzzling into place
of the overcast sky.

3. When I harbor a notion,
that child of a notion
had better behave.

Perhaps
Autumn gold.
The affluent river.

The application
is
the explication.

Leaf after leaf,
I am embracing
Prodigal sun.

EARLY FROST

I wake into the old world.
You are gone.
You have disappeared
through the crevice
of night.

A butterfly divides the forest.
The yellow remainder.

Winds blow.

In winter
we are schooled
in intricacies of branch.

All else,
all that lies
outside the
sumi-e of this,
is lightly sketched

so that the fundamentals
may be put in bold.

Then the snow
where the moment is
the moment magnified,
whited-out
into the light.

PART III

A Rough Draft

A ROUGH DRAFT

Darkness sits
on its prickly light.
The wind blows
every which way.
What will be hatching?
Never mind.
The body is a bay leaf.
We will stew
whatever comes.

The "I" as a flaw
through which we see
the entire landscape—
the hills at odds or even
with banks of cloud, the river of light.

A bird breaks out into the moment
as if the day were just another eggshell.

The mind is a sore breast full of milk.

MY SLEEVE

Child, the sonnet is itself a skeleton
Down to the bare bone, down to the bare bone
And skitters from idea to source, to spring
Open unexpectedly—from Nothing
Or from another world, borne, an infant
As he touches my sleeve describing an arc
That continues and that everyday life will hone—
Here on the changing table, trying, as I work,
To keep him down while not appearing to,
Again a sweep, then a coy glance (me too!)
As he nabs my sleeve. We have a secret pact
About beauty. The world's colors are shared
With all, but only he to the world gives back
Shy intimate wonder, his joy laid bare.

THE MOVE TOWARDS WINTER

I walked through evidence of love—
Autumn's embrace of summer—
Its truth shattering; it's brilliance
far fetched as a lone leaf turning
in the wind, fragile and urgent:
this light, this death, this love, this dark.

I have not thrown my cares
sufficiently to the winds.
I'm tired of carrying
on my back
that thorn of a plant
that grew so calligraphic.

In youth, there are crowds within.
Chatter, and a thousand birds speak.
While you and I've grown old
and hard to know
—all the paths we've taken,
turning us to stone.

THE CARDINAL

It seems foreign to Spring,
this sharp dominant call,

but there it is, right at the heart
of an April afternoon.

Meanwhile, over-the-wall beauty
of the horizontal cherry

in full blossom
gives way to that mimicry

of snow on a branch
that Tsurayuki spoke of

in his 31 syllables
as the flowers soften

and the branches begin to leave.

SPIN CYCLE

Spring will stir at each point
where winter sticks her needle.

*

Day agitates and agitates
until the colors run.

*

Every leaf joins the People's Army
in July, but by October is lost

in the Capital of Color,
running rampant, investing

every corner of the earth
with gold, vermilion.

*

Winter escapes, the warning shot
of Autumn still crackling in the air.

*

The cold divides and subdivides its territory
until all that is left is at stake.

APPROACH

1. When I was born
   the world was quiet.
   You had not entered
   with your magnifying glass.

   I am out on a limb.
   You sit there with me
   like a craze of light.

2. Compositionally,
     we are drawn apart;

   the simplest of breezes
   brushes through
      and against

   the acquilinity of line.

   Witness this destruction!
     the soberest curve
        of my body

   This is after the fact.
   Time collapses
     into a vertigo.

THE GOD OF THE LITERAL

Can your words medicate meaning?
   —your intonation pale
   —your intonation feverish.

      I inhabit only
      the enduring settlement
      of your remark.

I am not the rebel snow
come to take your lands
—what the clouds
stole across the sky
and gathered.

      More and more
      the afternoon
      is a trellis
      where shadows
      curl and cling.

All this Being - Counterfeit.
The god of the literal
pastes his stamp.

      We will find a small cafe.
      That's the part
      when we're together.
      But where will I fit
      when I am the jagged shape of loneliness?

I WRITE BACK

I

I write back to you
in the middle of my night
when all that comes to light
is dark,
and puzzling
The mind can, cannot re-form.

II

Mirroring
the toss
of an orange, love,
and pinks
to the sky
at dawn or dusk

held in suspense, dreamlike
in its capacity
the mind's center of gravity.

III

Can I not
take back
or be taken aback
by you?
All this is bull
I bull my way into the ring.

The angel is a red flag.
I wrestle with it.

Why am I pontificating?
Am I a dream?

IV

Dreams re-form
 (I come and go like one...)
Is a dream immortal?

They leave behind no body
and they sometimes come back to life.

V

Our real life
the experience of
the multiple 'I.'

VI

The self, a simple dream
that throws itself
into the future—

VII

Am I essentially a dream?

What then will be put into my grave?
 My marriage with the earth?
(and sky of course, yes sky)
union with all, quarks
and microbes, and all that enters
through the door of the senses?

Light glitters on the leaf.

VIII

Or, quite differently, am I a dream

in the mind of another?

The poster bed creaks.
(it's form is re-formation.)

Come, and as dreams, let us dissolve
one into the other

propagate

so that the sleep of the gods
does not grow tedious.

SOLID GROUND

The wind spills through the leaves
differently here; low hills

lie shadowed along the horizon
in strips like crinkled kelp.

Here the moon makes
an open breast of the night.

There are days I dive below
the horizon of our talk—

on the other side is a further
world, calm, unpeopled.

In the stagger-dance of the swallows
repositioning, I wake

from my thoughts of you—to
spread the ball of my foot

on solid ground.
Why, like cloud

following cloud
across the sky

do we empty
into each other this way?

ONE BY ONE

Individually we are like
thoughts born out of a brain,

we come and go. We harbor.

We make waves.

     *

We blink in
and out of existence
like particles.

     *

Are we mentally all one being,
—like a field of mushrooms?

     *

Divinity, an interaction.
—Part and whole in an embrace.

     *

Does our
consciousness
divide us or hold
us together?

I no longer know
what it is
to multiply or divide.

To accrue or land askew.

A SET OF WAVES IN AN OCEAN OF WAVES

 We are of the same substance,
but in the arms of this ocean,
what role do we play?
Where do we get the quiver? the quaver?

Clearly we somehow pluck the strings.
But under whose direction?

Is it not the voice of the sea?

      *

Asleep, we have no sense of waking realities
and yet that is what we do.

We wake realities.
It is our post.
Our office.

We probe, and they appear
like a herd of wild deer leaping in a meadow.

      *

The world we are sworn to
is telling us our story,

This night and day
off-and-on-existence

is the dotted line
we sign on to,
by being born.

It is the
firefly light
by which we sense
the world.

SPLIT SECOND PROPHECY

My love, you are a wild goose.
The sky says 'Sweet, I am myself today.

Look to the trees for your tea leaves.'
There where the maples meet

with the pines in a fine mesh of branch
I see wind, histories of wind—

And then wild geese, actual geese fly by.
Does the future fall back into us? Are we where

the winds of fates begin? Or where they settle?
Are we a bank of memories

some small boat brushes into?
Or do we call the gods back from

their future lodgings? Are we
a disturbance? A shaking awake?

I beg for, I long for the light of the sun.
The world is one split second behind me.

Are we a time machine with which
The gods walk backwards?

Or with which the gods walk
backwards into themselves?

Mind over matter, matters not a whit.
You, my wild goose, are the gist of it.

PART IV

What Lies in Store

WHAT LIES IN STORE

You talk circles
around me.

I am a pebble,
thrown into a pool.

Here among the reeds
the herons step,

but I am lost to these.

        All that the little bird
        told…

        —a wing flash
        through the leaves…

In the oligarchy of days
which is the richest?

The Past is a bath.
The Future

 bursts in.
The Moment

is still naked
in surprise.

        Idle Talk.
        But you tremble…
        …Even in the domestic light
        of all I have prepared for you:

        Your Coral Undergown? Your Ash Brocade?

(undercover of mist)

Your remarks
are terraced:

I cultivate them,
 then abandon the harvest
for the mountain goat's domain.

With careful steps
I extricate my way.

          The squared-off stem,
          the wild flowering
          of this burning bush,
          its leaves as red
          as a serpent's tongue.

CLOSE THE CURTAIN QUICKLY

Close the curtain quickly
while the day is still drawing
with its soft grey patches

—quickly, before the colors splay

or the patterned cloth
of our lives
will be unpinned.

We have come through
the open scissors of the day.

APRIL

The body of winter
is laid out
in the parlor
of spring.

We are quiet.
We are guests,
not members
of the family.

In a back room
they are reading his will.

You and I whisper
that the old man's
ink drawings
now are smudged.
We remember
how he used
to draw in his heyday
"Like drawing water
from a well,"
we would say,
surprised at some
fresh placement
of branch.

But even then
there were hints
of the flamboyance
that marked
his later years,
a dogwood blossom,
fallen on the step,
given the shape
of a bee,
for instance.

QUOTATIONS

The Waking have one common world
But the sleeping turn aside
Each into a world of his own.

I sent this quote from Heraclitus to my sister
who studies ancient philosophy and whose husband
is getting old and suffering from undefined ailments.

Yes, she wrote back and then there is Larry
who incorporates dreams into waking life
and insists on me answering the questions
raised in his dreams.

'Why are you bringing me
this plate of food?'
he'll demand loudly at night,
or 'What shall I do
with this jar I'm holding?'
Or, 'What am I supposed to do
with these tiles? (There are no tiles,
you are dreaming)

'Well what am I
supposed to do in my dream
                with these tiles?'

LIGHT TO THE SIDE OF, THEN IN FRONT OF THE EASEL

i.

Light is sitting
for its portrait.

We are drawing it
out with our shadows.

All of us—
even the holly bush—

participate fully.
There is nothing

we withhold.
And nothing we present.

The light is
its own presentation.

ii.

Light puts us to the easel.
We are surprised.

We feel sensitive,
and weathered, porous,

easily framed.
We are curious, and

all becomes extreme,
now that we are medium.

Light, brushes in hand
—why does it impress us

now, right now, with its
delicate, grave choices?

FEBRUARY IN JERSEY

1

Each day, you end as you begin:
stepping into another garment.
Perhaps the dressmakers battle.

And yet the scene is one of peace.
The old world is changing shape.

Skaters cut out a map
on ice for my thought to follow.
Thirsty shapes. As borders rearrange,

the old world includes
iced coffee, the year of the dog,

the steady trucking of complaint.
With each roll of the bolt
the material past lengthens.

2

Balance! Screams the sideways
location of self. Your words are florid,

orchidose. Each thought
comes out red and yelling,
like a baby.

The buzzard air picks
at the body of snow.

Life rebels against the forms.
You have brought me up
too far, it says.
I am not a happy medium.

Perhaps the dressmakers battle.
Yet the scene is one of peace.

3

Each day
you end as you begin,
stepping into
another garment.

How am I
to follow you?

In the whirl
and blossom
this spoke:
your carriage.

As in the language
of multiples

The wheel of three
and three and three—
and all it carries.

4

In verse, the infant Spring.
A particular complaint.

And then, motility.
In the sky's cumulus
all is pre and post

and new wave.
The garment of the day

becomes itself,
stretches out
until the evening change.

One arm begins to press
into the sleeve of night.

OUT OF DOORS

Two short trills and five long ones
The filled out form
Signatures spilling onto the page
And then the darting to and fro
A flight cut short by sycamore tree
By bridal veil, blackberry bush,
The splice of day and night that is the iris

HANIWA: *Hollow, clay figures found in*
Japanese burial mounds from 2500 years ago

1: Earthly Geometries

The sea is a fabric
that unravels
at the hem.

*

Only the Great Equator
remains the same.

And he lies, oh how he lies
at the center of things.

*

The world is fertile.

Incestuous, too.
…Body, giving birth
with soul to mind.

Body giving birth
with mind to word.

*

Behind the haniwa's eyes
is pure depth of field—

"Are you stealing motions
from the universe?"

2: Five Songs from the Burial Mounds

"Some Haniwa have bodies, swords,
carefully made of clay—"

> Don't tax me with your talk of the real.
> I'm from the underworld,
> what survives in you
> when nothing else survives.
>
> I am content in this existence.
> I want to be here where light
> draws smoke into knots it teasingly unravels.
>
> Don't tax me with the everyday.

> *

The Haniwa just don't know
what we've gone through
the last millennia.

They feel we have an edge.
And a soft spot.
Maybe they think
we're about to emerge
from the womb.

but what world awaits?
what world awaits?

Why, while dying, are we tied so
to the body—

> I am a low note.
> Don't trouble me with treble.

> *

There is an underworld lure
—a fisherman's folly…

    All is set.
    We meet at dawn.
    the line intact—

In the burial mound,
the keyhole-shaped burial mound.

             *

Night is a battlefield.
Mind, a temporary encampment.
Why does it hold me in thrall?

    And I would celebrate,
    if I could celebrate…
    But you keep falling back…
    You forget that you forget…

Night toggles into dream.

LIVIU CIULI, DIRECTOR

I had seen Coriolanus
four times in a row,
and was mesmerized by it.
—the orchestration
of crowds, in particular.

There was also a short scene
in which an old man
played the part of a servant,
but played it so well,
against the instincts of the line,

("Madam, the Lady Valeria
is come to visit you" he said,
with a tired voice, as if
he had his own life to lead,
a context to come out of)

that it seemed to hold the secret
of the whole play within it.
For a month or two
I carried the director's name
on the tip of my tongue.

Then I forgot, but
(because of that?) he
followed me back to
everyday life. He orchestrated
day after day just for me.

I'd see a man
on a street corner, or
 three people walking up a hill
and think "my director
has cast these people well."

One day a Brueghel painting

where an ordinary corner
used to be. Another day,
waiters with the motions
of flies—Eventually

I began to think
he orchestrated the sky.
And one day he orchestrated
the waves as they poured
onto the sand

—leaving behind beasts
and human caricatures
which I caught with my camera
before the sun
dried them away.

THE ONE AND THE MANY

All of the gods are present in any moment.
The god of the stern, the god of the lee.
Starboard and bow.

Sometimes the stern
steps forward unexpectedly.

*

The body lectures
to the heart's dismay.
The sky crosses itself.

*

I would have you
be like a wind
at the head of inquiry.
But you would have yourself be
"onto something"
Such is the desire of a wind.

*

The colors gather into white.
White dismembers them.

Light sends forth its shoots into black,
to get the colors back. And they come out:
coral, and the many inks.

BEAUTY, THAT RESTLESS GUARDIAN

Love: its truth is under-foot;
each leaf, the shy marriage bed
of light and death,
the choral and the bronze.

You have been whispering
to me along the sidewalks,
along the cracks:
along that emerald pathway of the moss.

Beauty can be out there.
Beauty can be in your face.

You and I are St. Mark's Square.

Love, and the flutter of love
in a sky full of pigeons.

PHAETHON'S HALF SISTER

All day I tend
my father's horses,
not daring to
ride across the skies.

To the Victor
belong the grasses,
the earth
he has sped over.

Oh my sweet,
my distant earth.
What is it
in your cold revolutions

that draws you
into my circle?
So much is lost
because I could not

be the keeper of it.
At home, I ponder
what fills the voices
not of other gods,

but of women and men..
Beauty grows like lichen.
I am carried from phrase
to phrase like water

over rock. The world
has become such a rich tapestry
that to move, anywhere,
is to tear fabric.

APOLOGY ACCEPTED

1.

You begin again
—a mind, used
to holding
itself at bay.

Only the sea
with its glaring
imperfection
can hold the shifting

weight of light
and cast no shadow
except in its
perennial margin.

I look over your letter
of apology,
stealing phrases
where appropriate.

2.

In the end
I cannot help
but admire:
you are persistent

and not without
eloquence. The oyster
rules his shell with
a mother-of-pearl hand.

The sun reconciles
with the leaves
after a long

dark argument.

The sea turns, beside itself
with envy. The moon,
in its own quarter,
slowly diminishes.

3.

You stash away
papers, bits
of currency,
the odd eraser.

Summer, urged on
by another theme
—an overwhelming
sense of color,

exists in another
measure, shored,
levied,
a tax over all.

A quiver of wind.
Somewhere along
the waters, Rain
has lost its pelt.

4.

Think of the orbits
slowly reflected
in the waters' swirl.
We are binary systems.

At any given moment

in our orbit
we are curving in towards
and drawn tangentially

away from the other.
and what we know
of each other
is clarified

and is distorted
equally
as we pass,
pulled in, drawn out...

ACKNOWLEDGMENTS

Part 1:

US 1 Volume 46/47 2003 (30th Anniversary Volume) "Marie-Eve"
   (called "On Dream" in this manuscript)
US 1 Volume 57 2012 "Moods and Confrontations"
US 1 Volume 62 2016 "Sunrise"
US 1 Volume 28-29 1993 "The Open Sleeve of Love"
US 1 Volume 34/35 1997 "Subject Matters"
US 1 Volume 61 2016 "Falcon Heart" (*nominated for Pushcart*)

Part II:
Archae 4 1992-3 "October"
US ! Volume 40/41 1999 "The Turning Over of the Earth"
US 1 Volume 55 2010 "Early Frost" (*in an earlier version*)

Part III:

Archae 4 1992-3 "Solid Ground"
US1 Volume 59 2014 "The Cardinal"
US! Volume 63 2018 "The Move Towards Winter"

Part IV:

gsu review spring/summer 2007 (Published as Finalist in Poetry
   Contest. Journal now called *New South*) "February in Jersey"

US 1 Volume 42/43 2000 "Close the Curtain Quickly"
US 1 Volume 38/39 1998 "April"
US 1 Volume 58 2012 (40th Anniversary Volume) "Quotations"
US 1 Volume 57 2011 "Phaethon's Half Sister"

I would like to acknowledge the enormous help I have received from US1 members and those attending the Long Poems Gatherings: Frederick Tibbetts, Winifred Hughes, Lois Marie Harrod, Elizabeth Socolow and David Herrstrom. Their work as well delights and sustains me. I am in awe of them all.

A special debt as well to my sister, the philosopher Ruth Saunders for (though she lives 1000 miles away) her almost daily discussions and a rare and far-reaching insight.

When she was 16, **Emily Saunders Nguyen** spent a year with a Japanese family in Kyoto, Japan. Later, she became interested in the waka, a short Classical Japanese form, and particularly in poems found in the seasonal poems of the Kokinshu (c. 905) and Shinkokinshu (c. 1201). The fusion of human feeling and a strong identity with natural elements is very prominent in these poems.

She is much indebted to Ki no Tsurayuki and his fellow compilors for their sense of ordering poems through loose narrative and love stories—stories that often end badly.

From the West, Jorge Luis Borges and Paul Valery made an early impression on her. Recently, Transtromer, Herrstrom, Tibbetts—who also fashion out of their contact with East and West new poetic forms.

She was born in Madison, Wisconsin. She is married to Hien Nguyen, born in Saigon, Vietnam. They have 3 sons, all of them very active in the creative world. Family interactions and discussion often center around creative endeavors. Phong, the youngest, is author of the novel *The Adventures of Joe Harper.* He is currently working on a work of historical fiction about 3rd century Vietnam. Nam, the second son is an Artist, Song-writer and Performer. Hoai, the oldest, does most of his writing in code! But beautiful jazz melodies come out of his fingers...

Emily is surrounded as well by creative daughter-in-laws. Sarah Nguyen and Samantha Tessler Nguyen are both artists. Gwendolyn Smith Nguyen is a Cellist. Everywhere, people with new ideas to proffer and relate.

Family has always been important. Her parents, sister and brothers, were all interested in the diverse things the world had to offer, and in the workings and wanderings of the mind. At times, she had a hard time getting a word in edgewise! She loved the lively exchange of ideas.

Emily lived in Montreal for 6 years and taught at Vanier College there. She is like a patch of trumpet vines, her old and new roots spread here and there.

www.ingramcontent.com/pod-product-compliance
Lightning Source LLC
Chambersburg PA
CBHW021154090426
42740CB00008B/1081